The B|G Man

My Story

PHIL WEAVER

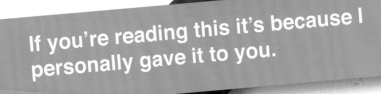

If you're reading this it's because I personally gave it to you.

Why have I given it to you?

Because I have a story to tell you.

I can hardly believe some of the things that have happened to me over the years but I wonder what you will think of it all.

So here it is...
...this is my story

I LOVE TO ASK PEOPLE to try and guess what I do for a living. They look at my 6ft 5in and 35 stone frame and come up with some pretty fascinating answers. They guess everything from sumo wrestler, strong man and bouncer to opera singer, actor, accountant, solicitor and everything in between. I wonder what you thought I did when you first met me? One thing is for sure, few say ballet dancer – the thought of me in a tutu really doesn't bear thinking about, believe me!

WELL, I'M ACTUALLY A NUMBER of things – a motivational speaker and communicator, an author, and I also like to think of myself as a bit of an entertainer as well - however, few rarely believe I am telling the truth when I tell them what I really do.

'Never in a millions years!' they say - 'you just don't look like one.'

So what am I?

Well, believe it or not, I'm a church minister, a preacher, or what some people might call, the vicar. To be honest I'm thrilled I don't fit the stereotypical idea of what most people think a minister looks like. Actually I've been in the ministry over 35 years – but my story began well before I entered the ministry.

BIG DAY
BIG FAMILY

CERTIFICATE

1 & 2 ELIZ. 2 CH. 20

Name and Surname...... Philip Charles Weaver

Sex...... Boy

Date of Birth...... Twenty Ninth December 1957

Place of Birth { Registration District...... Stoke on Trent

Sub-district......

Superintendent Reg

I, ... Registrar ...... District of ...... STOKE-ON-TRENT ...... do h

...... particu ...... have been compiled from an en

DECEMBER 29, 1957 WAS A big day for
me. It was the day I made my grand entrance into the
world. It was the day Philip Charles Weaver was born.
It all happened in the bedroom of a council house in
the Potteries.

OUR FAMILY WAS A FAIRLY big family – with mum and dad there were 7 of us in all. Mum and dad always worked hard to make ends meet and to provide for us. We certainly weren't rich by any means, but then again, neither were we poor – just a normal family doing the best they could to get by – just like many other families in the industrial potbank city of Stoke-on-Trent.

BIG DREAMS
BIG HEAD

I SUPPOSE LIKE EVERY KID I had big dreams of becoming a professional footballer or making it big in some way and becoming rich and famous. In fact there was only one thing that prevented me from doing this – and that was 'talent' – or should I say the lack of it! I wasn't particularly talented at anything. I never shone at school; I wasn't exceptional in any subjects. In fact, the only thing I was good at in school was 'lunch - oh, and a bit of sport.'

ONE TEACHER WROTE ON MY report 'Last year Philip hit rock bottom. This year he started drilling!' To be honest I didn't think I was that bad, but at best I was just an average, or more often than not slightly below average, type of kid.

CITY OF STOKE-ON-TRENT EDUCATION COMMITTEE

CARMOUNTSIDE
JUNIOR HIGH SCHOOL

REPORT BOOK

NAME *Philip Weaver*

HOWEVER, WHAT I WAS THOUGH, looking back was a bit of a 'big head' and definitely a 'big mouth.' In truth, it was all just impetuous bravado that veiled a rather insecure, lonely lad who was trying to gain approval but lacked in confidence because of his general inability, poor self-worth and an embarrassing speech impediment. As you can imagine growing up on a tough council estate in the Midlands just wasn't the place to show too much vulnerability. I learnt to hold my own, even though it was all bluster! So I acted like Billy big boots when I was with my mates.

I CAN SEE NOW HOW I could have so easily been led astray and gone down the wrong road. It doesn't bear thinking about where I might have ended up! I thank God – I really do – because I can see He had His hand on me from a very early age.

BIG HELP
BIG INFLUENCE

I WOULD HAVE BEEN AROUND 12 and I was playing football with one of my mates in the street. I loved football and having a kick-about. I played whenever I could – at school, at weekends, every evening. I also played for the church – St Johns at the top of our road. I was the junior goalkeeper. Sometimes if they were short of a keeper I'd get a game for the seniors as well. However, there was a rub – to play for the church on a Saturday, you had to go to the young people's bible class on the previous Sunday. That's where I met Roy Phillips, the vicar.

ROY WAS IN HIS EARLY 30s and at the time he had a wife and three young children. I liked Mr Phillips – I liked him a lot. He always seemed to have a lot of time for me. It felt like he was really interested in how I was doing. He was a great encourager and he had the knack of making me feel special. There was something about him that was different and I remember he spoke about God and Jesus as if he knew them personally and as if they helped him all the time. Looking back there's no doubt Roy Phillips had a major influence on my life - something I am still, even to this day, very grateful for.

BIG SHOCK
BIG UPSET

ANYWAY, AS I WAS SAYING, I was having a kick-about with my mate on his street at the other end of the estate. It was about 6.30pm and suddenly he just came out with it …'hey Phil, what about the vicar at the church?'

'What about him?' I said.

'Oh, I thought you would have heard – he died today.'

His words stopped me right in my tracks.

'What!' I said. 'Hey, don't joke about things like that! Mr Phillips can't have died, not at his age. Anyway I only saw him on Sunday and he was alright then. You must have got it wrong.'

'No honestly mate,' he said, 'everyone's talking about it.'

'I'VE GOT TO GO,' I said, and then I ran and I ran as fast as my little legs could carry me. 10 minutes later I arrived outside the vicarage at St Johns. It was true – he had died. I couldn't believe it. It was a massive shock and it upset me big time. I was only young, and I just couldn't take it all in.

MR PHILLIPS WAS THE FIRST person I really knew who had died. For the first time I felt pain deep inside of me, the type of pain that only a real sense of loss can bring. I wasn't to know at the time but such indescribable pain only ten thousand times worse would invade the very core of my being some 40 years later.

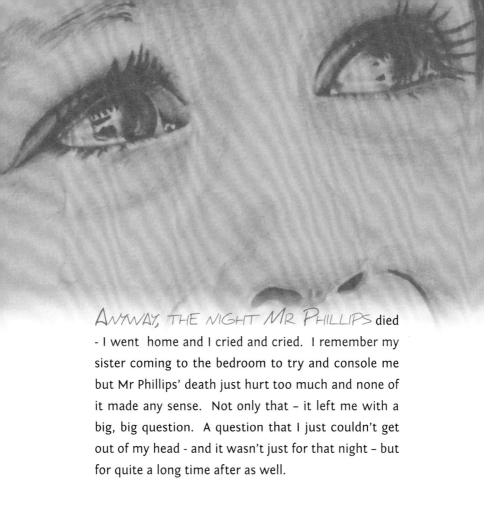

ANYWAY, THE NIGHT MR PHILLIPS died - I went home and I cried and cried. I remember my sister coming to the bedroom to try and console me but Mr Phillips' death just hurt too much and none of it made any sense. Not only that – it left me with a big, big question. A question that I just couldn't get out of my head - and it wasn't just for that night – but for quite a long time after as well.

THE QUESTION THAT KEPT going around my mind was this ...

'What would happen to me if I suddenly died? Would I go to Heaven or would I go someplace else?'

I must admit I really didn't have a clue and it concerned me. Even at such a tender age - I was scared of dying. I don't know why but I was and it was very real, and after what had happened to Roy Phillips who was so young, I couldn't help but worry about it all the more.

NO MATTER HOW HARD I tried I just couldn't shake it. For some reason It was something that refused to go away. Incidently, I'm sure it's a question that also haunts many others as well. Sure they like to think all will be okay when they die but nevertheless, they still have that big question lurking at the back of their minds ... *'what if?'*

what **if...**

BIG MOVE
BIG INVITATION

NOT LONG AFTER WE MOVED home to a place about three miles away from our old house. It was a big move for the Weaver family.

One day about 18 months or so later I was walking to school and as usual I met my older cousin walking in the opposite direction to college. In many ways it was no different to any other day. We would meet most mornings and stop to talk for a couple of minutes before we continued on our separate ways. But on this particular morning he told me he had bought me a ticket to accompany him to a Christian gig on the following Saturday evening. It was to take place at the church – St Johns – and he really hoped I'd be able to make it.

I MUST ADMIT I DIDN'T really want to go but how could I say, 'thanks but no thanks.' After all he had paid for the ticket!

'Okay, thanks,' I found myself saying. 'What time?'

'7.30,' he said. 'Meet me outside the church at 7.'

Although in some ways it was the last thing I wanted to do, I ended up going and boy am I glad that I did. It ended up being a 'red letter' day for me, one that would literally change my life forever.

BIG CHANGE
BIG IMPRESSION

I ENJOYED THAT SATURDAY EVENING.
The concert was packed with wall to wall people and
the atmosphere was buzzing. I was made to feel really
welcome. And as for the music, it was good. There
was a real mix of rock and roll, R & B, folk, and a touch
of classical thrown in for good measure.

HOWEVER, THE THING THAT really made a big impression on me was the people. In particular, the lads I used to play football with. There was definitely something different about them. They had changed. Something had clearly happened to them since I last knew them. One thing was for sure, whatever it was, I didn't have it. Yet for some strange reason, I knew I wanted it. Then I discovered it wasn't an 'it' at all, it was a person.

DURING THE INTERVAL AND AT the end of the concert I talked to a few of the guys to try and grasp what had happened to them. One after another shared with me how they'd become Christians. One in particular, Alan, told me his story of how he had come to put His trust in the Lord Jesus Christ through a mission held by the American evangelist - Billy Graham. He told me how he felt his life had totally changed as a result. Then he asked me something that really hit a tender spot and rang a few alarm bells.

'Hey Phil, what would happen to you if you died tonight? Do you know where you'd end up?'

'IT'S FUNNY YOU'VE ASKED THAT,' I said, and I told him about my very real fear of dying, which hadn't left me. Alan then went on to explain how the Bible shows that the only way to get to Heaven is through receiving Jesus Christ into your life and by making Him your personal Lord and Saviour.

'How do you do that?' I asked.

'Well, it all begins by turning to Him and inviting the Lord Jesus Christ into your heart,' he answered. I remember being impressed by what he'd said and he told me this is what had brought about the change that I could see in so many of the lads' lives.

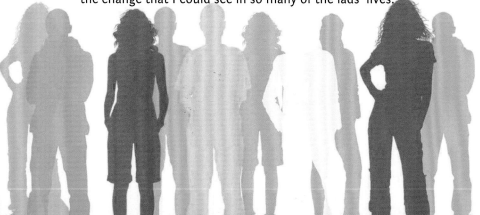

BIG MOMENT
BIG DECISION

THAT NIGHT I WENT HOME on the bus. As I waited at the bus stop I couldn't help thinking about what Alan had been telling me. The funny thing was I wasn't even sure I believed in a God at the time. But I simply couldn't get away from the fact of so many changed lives that I had just witnessed with my own eyes. I got on the bus and headed for the back of the top deck. There was only a handful of folk on the bus and only me upstairs.

Now on that short journey, after paying the conductor and getting my ticket, I remember saying to myself in a sort of made up prayer ... 'Lord Jesus Christ if you do exist and can change my life for the better and if you are the only one who can provide me with a ticket to Heaven and give me eternal life, then I want you in my life. So I'm inviting you to come into my life to be my Lord and Saviour, to live with me and to help me. Amen.'

BIG NEW START
BIG ADVENTURE

Now I'm not sure what I expected to happen on the bus that night when I prayed, but this I do know, in that very moment something did happen deep inside of me. I knew I'd made a big decision, even though I didn't understand it all at the time. Let me tell you, I have no doubt whatsoever that the Lord Jesus Christ did come into my life in response to my garbled invitation. In fact, I know this will sound a bit cheesy – but I genuinely believe that night I got on the bus one person and got off the bus another. That's exactly the way it felt. It was as if I got on the bus without God and got off that No. 39 double decker with God. It was as simple as that - and I just knew it.

SOMETHING DEFINITELY HAPPENED THAT night and I can honestly say my life began to change and I could see and feel those changes. At first they were small but they were definitely there and in time they were evident for all to see. In fact, in time, it became clear I'd changed in most areas of my life. It was as if I'd had a fresh start – and in truth I had – the Bible actually describes it as being 'born again.'

BIG ASK
BIG SURPRISE

I KNOW I WAS YOUNG but right from the outset I felt God just wanted to speak to me.

Now what happened to me that very same week also took me by surprise. I fully appreciate that I was only in my mid-teens – but I couldn't get the thought out of my head that at sometime in the future God wanted me to work for Him in some kind of 'full-time' service type of way. But never in my wildest dreams did I think He might want me to eventually become a Church Minister.

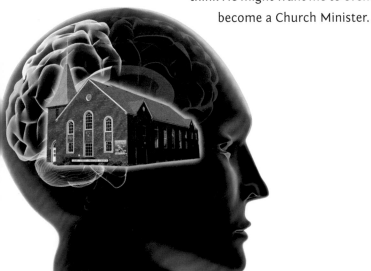

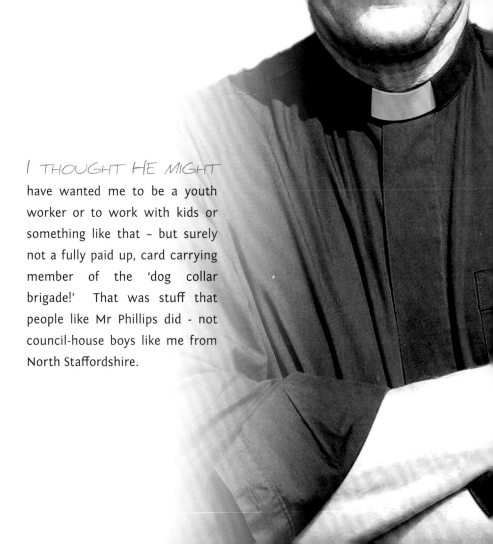

I THOUGHT HE MIGHT have wanted me to be a youth worker or to work with kids or something like that – but surely not a fully paid up, card carrying member of the 'dog collar brigade!' That was stuff that people like Mr Phillips did - not council-house boys like me from North Staffordshire.

NEVERTHELESS, I FELT really sure that God was calling me in some way – whatever that meant! This thought never left me and I knew one day it would become a reality – how? I hadn't got a clue – but I do know that God was on my case and He was wanting me to take seriously what He was asking me to do.

A YEAR OR SO LATER I left school with virtually no qualifications and quickly went through a number of jobs. To be honest, I didn't enjoy any of them in particular and if the truth be known, I didn't keep any of them very long either. I guess there was only one thing I really wanted – and that was to train somewhere to follow what I thought God had asked me to do, even though I wasn't sure what that was at the time. It was never going to be easy, especially as I had no exam results to back me up. But then again one thing I have learnt over the years is that God specialises in making a way where there seems to be no way. And this is exactly what He did for me.

ANYWAY, A COUPLE OF YEARS later, quite amazingly God did make a way and I found myself going off to Bible College in Birmingham to read theology. There I trained for three years and it was there I met a girl from Scotland who would eventually become my wife (I certainly looked different back then didn't I)! It would be together that Helen and I would face the future and continue with our great big adventure in God – and in all honesty it's been an adventure that has never ended.

BIG CHALLENGE, BIG THINGS IN THE PIPELINE

STUDYING THEOLOGY IN A STRICT Bible College was always going to be taxing for a lad with no formal qualifications. To be frank, just living there was an enormous challenge in itself!

Up, washed and dressed by 6.25am and in bed for 10.30pm. A dress code of jacket shirt and tie had to be adhered to at all times. The three hourly supervised study periods every evening and the dozen or more different subjects studied every term seemed never-ending. With weekly mission placements to attend and the daily 'chore' requirements to fulfil along with a host of other things - well believe me, it was a serious culture shock! A million miles removed from student life as most people know it today!

THEN THERE WERE THE ACADEMIC and financial challenges I faced. You see when brains were given out I thought they said trains and it felt like I'd missed out completely!

On the money front, my parents simply weren't in a position to help with the fees and with the local education authority at first refusing to offer a grant - it proved to be a real test. However I knew God had called me and my faith was strong and I had no doubt that somehow He would get me through!

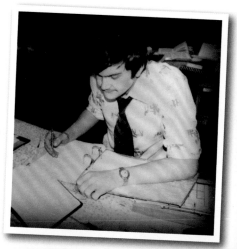

THREE YEARS LATER I COMPLETED my Bible College training. To everyone's surprise, including mine, I graduated and took my first fledgling steps into 'full time' probationary ministry. Suddenly I found myself at the age of 22, taking on my first church in the town of Runcorn in Cheshire. I was a real greenhorn and in truth I didn't have a clue what I was doing. I trusted God for everything - I had to!

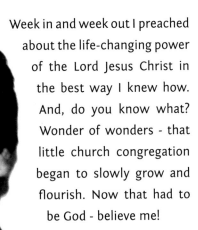

Week in and week out I preached about the life-changing power of the Lord Jesus Christ in the best way I knew how. And, do you know what? Wonder of wonders - that little church congregation began to slowly grow and flourish. Now that had to be God - believe me!

WE SAW THE LORD do some pretty amazing things back then and we saw Him really provide for us in many unexpected and miraculous ways. It was another three and a half years or more before I would successfully complete my ministry probation period. I was ordained on the 12th of May 1983. That was the day I officially became the 'Reverend Philip Charles Weaver.'

The Elim Church
Incorporated.

Certificate of Ordination.

This is to Certify that *Philip Charles Weaver* of Werrington Road, Bucknall, Stoke-on-Trent, Staffordshire has been ordained to the regular ministry in the denomination known as the Elim Church at Elim Conference, Clacton-on-Sea, Essex on the twelfth day of May in the year of our Lord One Thousand Nine Hundred and Eighty Three. Previous to this Ordination our Brother had given full proof of his calling to the ministry during his training and probationary period to the satisfaction of the Executive Presbytery. He is therefore hereby duly authorised to perform all the functions of his ministerial office.

We the undersigned being present at the request of the Executive Presbytery of the Elim Church acting in our official capacity as Ordained Ministers discharged our duties in connection therewith.

John Lancaster
Leuwewalen
John Wright

Officiating Ministers.

Dated and signed this twelfth day of May One Thousand Nine Hundred and Eighty Three in the year of our Lord

I have chosen and ordained you - John 15. 16.
Go ye therefore and teach all nations, baptizing them in the name of the Father, and of the Son, and of the Holy Ghost: Teaching them to observe all things whatsoever I have commanded you: and, lo, I am with you alway, even unto the end of the world.

IT HAD BEEN QUITE A JOURNEY over all. In fact six and a half years from the day I entered Bible College to the day I was ordained. Through it all God was good and He remained faithful to me and His Word in every way - just like He promised He would.

YOU SEE, THE LIVING GOD really can make a way where there seems to be no way - no matter who we are and no matter what situation we might find ourselves in. When everyone says 'it's impossible,' He says 'come on trust me - with me all things are possible!'

OVER THE YEARS I HAVE led churches in Cheshire, the Rhondda Valley in South Wales, the West Midlands, Leicestershire and Hertfordshire. Also for the best part of six years I was appointed as the Regional Superintendent (The Bishop) of The Metropolitan Regional area which encompassed London and the surrounding areas. In this role I oversaw a total of 130 church congregations and over 200 different ministers.

Who'd have thought it? Not me, that was for sure!

I'VE ALSO HAD THE JOY of starting and establishing a number of new churches around the country as well as spearheading a successful national community initiative. This involved over 1500 different church congregations and organisations at a cost of over £2.2m and was launched at Westminster.

Phew! I'm well and truly exhausted just thinking about it all! But God has been very good to us over the years and we feel truly blessed for what He has done and continues to do both in us and through us.

Now I guess you could be forgiven for thinking that life for me has been nothing but plain sailing - but, in truth I have found myself having to navigate through some real stormy times as well.

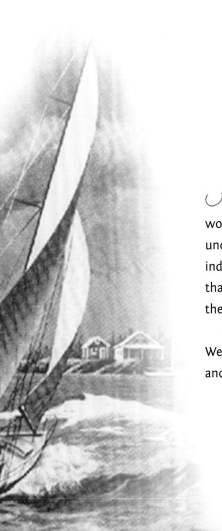

UNBEKNOWN TO US, we would soon sail headlong into some uncharted and very turbulent waters indeed. In fact into a force ten storm that threatened to severely shipwreck the Weaver family!

We were definitely going to need an anchor that would hold the boat firm.

BIG TOWN
BIG OPPORTUNITY

IN THE WINTER OF 1996 we had the opportunity as a family to move back to Leicestershire to the university and market town of Loughborough where we opened a new church. In fact we are still there today thrilled to be involved in building and growing this vibrant fellowship called New Springs City Church. What a buzz it is to see so many lives in our community being totally transformed by the Gospel power of the Lord Jesus Christ through the ministry of this amazing local church. I am so proud to be one of its leaders!

I HAVE FOUND THAT WHEN YOU accept Jesus Christ into your life making Him your Lord and Saviour you never know where He'll end up leading you and what He will actually accomplish through you. You just don't know what miracle He's going to perform next. I'm living proof of that!

New
Springs

HOWEVER, AS I SUGGESTED EARLIER it would be very wrong for me to intimate in any way that our strong Christian faith has made us somehow immune from the knocks, heartaches and hurts of life. We have certainly faced our fair share of trials – and through them all I believe God has seen us through - but at times it has been really tough. But by far the biggest trauma of all happened much more recently – in fact in the Summer of 2011. At the time Helen and I had been married for almost 33 years. What happened was our worst nightmare. In fact to be honest any parents worst nightmare.

BIG STORY
BIG TESTIMONY

My testimony is one where I am able to say how over the years I have proved God to be faithful and true to His Word in every situation I have found myself in. One thing is for sure though, God hasn't always done things the way I would have wanted Him to. But what I've learnt is that - in the long run He knows best. He knows what He is doing and He really does have our very best interests at heart.

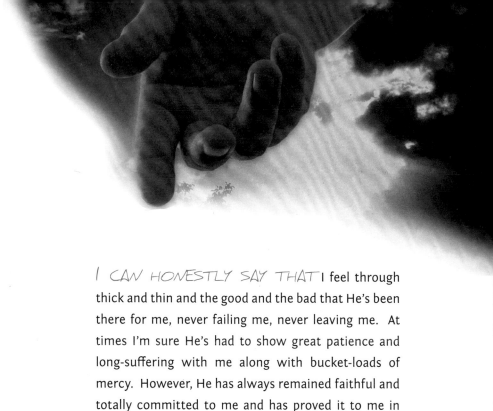

I CAN HONESTLY SAY THAT I feel through thick and thin and the good and the bad that He's been there for me, never failing me, never leaving me. At times I'm sure He's had to show great patience and long-suffering with me along with bucket-loads of mercy. However, He has always remained faithful and totally committed to me and has proved it to me in many ways and on many occasions.

BIG ISSUES
BIG PROBLEMS
BIG TRAUMA

WE HAVE FACED SOME PRETTY big problems in our time. I am talking big family issues, big financial difficulties, big health matters to cope with and some pretty big situations to deal with. There have been big mountains to climb and big obstacles to overcome – none more than the unexpected and sudden death of my youngest son Matthew in the Summer of 2011.

MATTHEW WAS ONLY 29 YEARS of age and left behind a beautiful wife and two wonderful young sons, one 6 and one just 4 years old. It was a crippling and devastating blow for all of us. One minute he had everything to live for, the next minute he was dead and gone. I will never forget how I felt the moment the doctor told us he had died. How could it be possible? Matt had only gone to the hospital that day for a routine medical procedure that should have taken no more than 15 minutes or so. However for one reason or another it never actually took place but as he was leaving the hospital to come back home he suddenly collapsed.

AFTER TAKING HIM TO THE resuscitation unit and doing all they could - Matt was pronounced dead shortly afterwards. The doctor told us and instantly shock and indescribable emotional pain ricocheted through every part of my mind and body. In a second every ounce of strength drained from me and it was as if time had been suspended in that very moment. Surely this wasn't happening to us.

It's hard to describe how I felt. If I thought I felt pain and hurt 40 years before, when Roy Phillips had died - then this was a billion times worse. The gut-wrenching pain I now felt was simply incomparable to anything else I'd ever felt in my life.

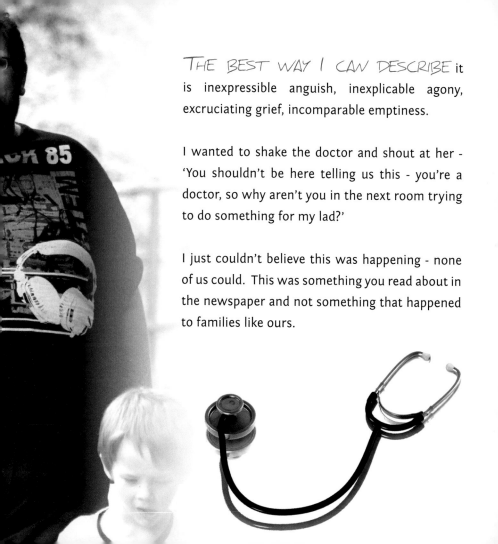

THE BEST WAY I CAN DESCRIBE it is inexpressible anguish, inexplicable agony, excruciating grief, incomparable emptiness.

I wanted to shake the doctor and shout at her - 'You shouldn't be here telling us this - you're a doctor, so why aren't you in the next room trying to do something for my lad?'

I just couldn't believe this was happening - none of us could. This was something you read about in the newspaper and not something that happened to families like ours.

As I STOOD IN THAT LITTLE hospital side room, trying to take it all in, with Sarah, Matt's young wife, Helen, and my other son Nathan, we just held one another in a wash of tears and disbelief.

I prayed, oh how I prayed that God would give him back to us - but it wasn't to be. As much as I didn't want it to be, God for one reason or another had decided this was Matt's time.

THE DAYS, WEEKS AND MONTHS that followed were an emotional roller coaster - a horrendous big dipper of a ride.

It is almost impossible to grasp what I am really talking about here. Losing a child as we did, not to mention being left to pick up the pieces thereafter is one of the most difficult emotional situations to ever have to face and get through. You really have to have gone through it to understand it - it's the type of pain and agony that no amount of words can begin to explain.

My Story

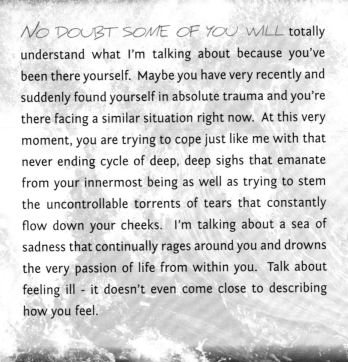

NO DOUBT SOME OF YOU WILL totally understand what I'm talking about because you've been there yourself. Maybe you have very recently and suddenly found yourself in absolute trauma and you're there facing a similar situation right now. At this very moment, you are trying to cope just like me with that never ending cycle of deep, deep sighs that emanate from your innermost being as well as trying to stem the uncontrollable torrents of tears that constantly flow down your cheeks. I'm talking about a sea of sadness that continually rages around you and drowns the very passion of life from within you. Talk about feeling ill - it doesn't even come close to describing how you feel.

And you just feel so spiritually, emotionally, mentally and physically exhausted.

You go to bed every night, eventually falling asleep with tears in your eyes, hoping you'll wake up in the morning to find that the whole episode has been nothing more than a dreadful nightmare. However, you wake up still exhausted, still with tears in your eyes, still with your head pounding and the real nightmare continues as you wonder how you're going to face another day.

BIG HEARTBREAK
BIG HEALER

ONE THING IS FOR SURE broken and shattered hearts are difficult to live with no matter who we are and no matter what we believe. In fact, in the natural, broken and shattered hearts are near on impossible to fix and put back together again. Sure, a doctor can give a person tablets that help suppress the emotional pain and that can help you to sleep - but at the end of the day when the effect wears off the broken and shattered heart remains and it's as painful as ever.

But did you know, that there is one who specialises in healing broken hearts - but sadly He is the last one that most people ever want to look to - His name is Jesus.

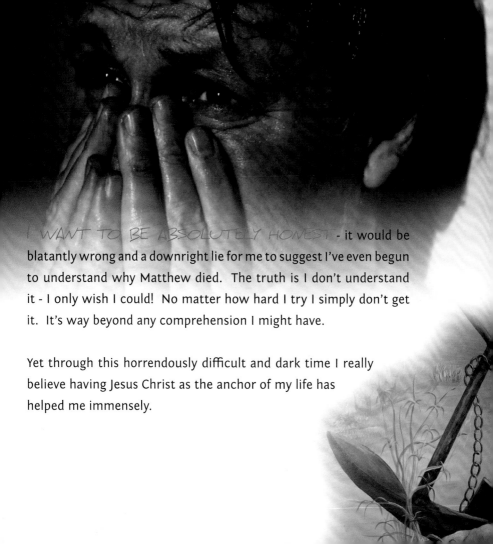

I WANT TO BE ABSOLUTELY HONEST - it would be blatantly wrong and a downright lie for me to suggest I've even begun to understand why Matthew died. The truth is I don't understand it - I only wish I could! No matter how hard I try I simply don't get it. It's way beyond any comprehension I might have.

Yet through this horrendously difficult and dark time I really believe having Jesus Christ as the anchor of my life has helped me immensely.

THE BIBLE DESCRIBES GOD AS A comforting God. One who is ready and willing to walk and support us through the tough and dark periods of life. Times that we all have to face from time to time. Times, that I guess are inevitable.

For me, I know without doubt that He has helped me and my family in many ways to battle and win through. Now don't get me wrong, it's no walk in the park - believe me, it isn't. Every single day is a big, big challenge, but I know I don't have to face it on my own. I know the Lord Jesus Christ is committed to walking the journey with me - all the way!

YOU KNOW ON ONE OCCASION Jesus actually said that one of the reasons He came was to heal the broken hearted. And in my experience there is no one else or anything else that can bring such healing. In another place in the Bible it tells us 'God is a very present and real help in times of trouble.' And though sometimes it is far from easy I have found this to be very much the case as well.

When Matt died the Weaver family was suddenly thrown into devastating turmoil. Yet we have found some real peace in it all as well. A type of peace the world can't give and a peace the world can't take away either. I am talking about the peace of God!

CLOSE BEREAVEMENT ALWAYS brings great pain and of course there's inconsolable grief and sorrow as well, but for me there's also been a peace.

For example, I am at total peace with where Matt is today. He also knew the Lord Jesus Christ as his Lord and Saviour. He trusted Jesus with his life and followed Him and today I have no doubt he is in Heaven.

In fact the Bible promises this. It says, anyone who has the Son of God (Jesus) in their life, then they will have eternal life and their place in Heaven is assured! (1 John 5:11)

Matt definitely made Jesus his Lord and Saviour and put his trust in Him, therefore his place in Heaven is guaranteed.

I AM ALSO AT PEACE WITH the fact that one day I shall definitely see him again and spend the whole of eternity with him - in that place where there's no more death and no more goodbyes to be said.

Of this fact I am absolutely certain and at peace about.

In truth, it's an assurance and a peace that only God can give.

I GUESS WE LIVE IN AN age when we can buy a piece of almost anything - a piece of bread, a piece of cake, a piece of cheese, a piece of pizza, a piece of all types of things. But do you know what, it doesn't matter where you go and it doesn't matter how much money you've got, you can never go and buy a piece of peace. Many have tried and many have failed to fill a void in their lives and take away the pain of all types of things that have happened to them. But in truth only Jesus, the Prince of Peace can give you real peace - no matter what you are going through, no matter what you are facing.

NOW MATT'S DEATH IS ONLY one part of the story. Agreed - it's a huge part and I've tried to explain how God has helped me through it. Yet there are so many good things that God has done in my life that if I were to tell you them all, I'm afraid you'd be here all week reading this here story of mine.

BIG MIRACLES
BIG GOD

THERE HAVE DEFINITELY BEEN SOME
pretty amazing highs over the years where our
walk with God is concerned. We have seen Him do
some truly mind blowing things and change many
situations that have seemed impossible. We have seen
Him answer so many prayers and perform so many
miracles and we have seen that there is just no end to
the extent of His love. Knowing Him is someone really
worth knowing. He really has proved over the years to
to be the closest companion.

His Royal Highness The Prince of Wales
requests the pleasure of the company of

Rev Philip Weaver

...ption for

WHAT YOU'VE READ IN THIS little booklet is just a snippet of my life so far. I haven't even mentioned the time when our house burnt down or when I ended up breaking a world record, resulting in me being invited to go to Clarence House to meet Prince Charles. Or, when I was rushed into hospital with life-threatening blood clots in several parts of my body and how the Lord got me through that one.

Then, of course, there are the tens of thousands of people that I have had the privilege to speak to, inspire and motivate around the world. And time doesn't allow me to share with you the many community and social initiatives I've had the joy of setting up, which included a national Christian initiative, which literally touched the nation. Then there are the half a dozen books I've had published and there is so much more to tell as well.

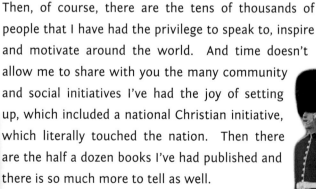

I told you that life for me with God had been a serious adventure - didn't I!

BY FAR, THE GREATEST THRILL of all is to not only see what God has done in my life, but to also have experienced how He has transformed untold numbers of other ordinary people's lives as well.

I have literally seen people healed, drug addicts and pushers delivered, marriages restored, families reconciled and men and women, both young and old, touched by the powerful hand of God. People whose lives were never the same again after they met with Jesus.

IT WAS NO DIFFERENT WHEN Jesus walked the earth.

Friends and strangers.
Beggars and soldiers.
Priests and prostitutes.
Rich and poor.
Singles and couples.

It didn't matter who they were Jesus had a way with people, an ability to see through the sometimes tangled mess of their lives and He knew what they needed most. The people He met back then were never the same again either.

THEIR STORIES AND MINE ALONG with multitudes of others, past and present - share a common thread - a life-changing encounter with Jesus.

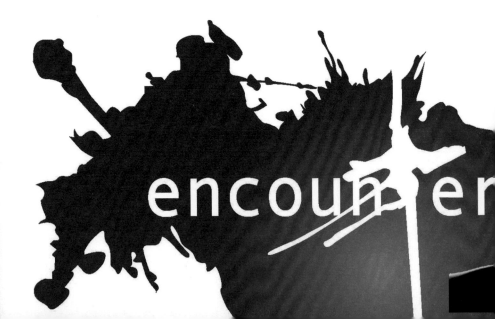

encoun er

AND SO THERE WE HAVE IT - just some of the highlights, and you might say the lowlights, of my story so far. And here I am three and a half or more decades later, still trusting God, still walking with Jesus, and believe it or not still enjoying the big adventure of knowing Him.

And do you know what? There is no reason whatsoever why you shouldn't get to know Him for yourself as well. You too can enter into and enjoy the amazing adventure and the plan that God has for your life.

It all begins by simply putting your trust in Him like I did all those years ago when I invited Him into my life to be my Lord and Saviour.

THE BIG QUESTION
THE BIG CHALLENGE

OBVIOUSLY I DON'T KNOW WHAT your situation is right now, I don't know what you're going through or what your life currently looks like at the moment. It could be good, it may be bad. But what I am sure about is this – that the God I believe in, this Jesus, I have talked and written about here, wants to be a part of your life and family. I know He wants to do you good. You have read about my life with its ups and downs. I can tell you it has been a heck of a rollercoaster. I'll admit, I haven't understood parts and I also admit I have brought some of my problems on myself through the wrong choices I have made. But the one thing I am absolutely certain of though, is that Jesus Christ has been a constant in my life; whether it's been through the good or through the bad times. I can honestly say that if it wasn't for my belief in Him I don't know where I would be today. Anyway, maybe it's time for you to put your trust in Him and experience the love of God for yourself.

THIS IS WHAT THE BIBLE SAYS: *'God loves you so much that He sent His only Son Jesus Christ to save you, that if you believe in Him you will not perish but have everlasting life.'* (John 3:16)

Now that's a massive promise and if it's true, it's too important for any of us to ignore.

I GUESS THERE ARE THREE **different types of response you could have after reading my story:**

1. You could say 'Well, that was interesting, but it's not for me.' Well, If that's you then that's fine. May I just say thanks for reading my story. Why not pass this booklet on to someone else who you think might enjoy reading it. I'd really appreciate that.

2. Or, you could be saying, 'This makes some kind of sense to me, and I'd like to know more.' If this is you, maybe you owe it to yourself to discover more about having a personal relationship with God through His Son Jesus. Why not check out an Alpha Course (alpha.org) near where you live, which will help you get to know Jesus for yourself. Or contact me via email - I'd love to chat with you more.

3. Or, you might say 'This has really spoken to me and I actually want to receive Jesus Christ into my life and trust Him with my future and eternal destiny, I really do want to start my personal adventure with God.'

The
BIG
Man
My Story

YOU CAN DO THIS BY SAYING and meaning this simple prayer –

Lord Jesus Christ, here I am, I can come no other way, so take me as I am. Thank you for loving me even though I haven't loved you. You know the things I have done which are not great and have not been pleasing in your eyes. I ask that you forgive me for all the selfish and sinful things that I have done, some of which are still in my life. Thank you for forgiving me and coming into my life. Help me now as I start over again, but this time with you at the centre. No longer am I going to go my own way. Today I am deciding to follow you by asking you to be my Saviour and Lord. Lord Jesus Christ, please send your Holy Spirit, to help me to know without doubt that you have come into my life. Amen.

Now, if you have said this prayer and meant it, I would like to say you have just made one of the best decisions you will ever make in your lifetime – Congratulations!

The BIG Man

I WOULD LOVE IT IF YOU could let me know that you prayed this prayer. Why? Because I would like to send you a booklet that will help you develop your new relationship with Christ Jesus (free of charge - no strings attached)!

Now of course, my story is ongoing and no doubt I'll still have to face some challenges in the future, but I'm determined to let God have His way in my life. To be honest it's exciting - I wonder where my adventure will take me next.

If you want to find out more about my life or if you have any questions about this God I've spoken about then I'd love you to get in touch with me. You can email me at phil@newsprings.org.uk

THANK YOU SO MUCH FOR taking the time to read my story. I trust you have found it a fascinating read. Hopefully you've even found it helpful in some way as well.

Well, whatever you do, take care.
Every blessing,
The Big Man

Phil Weaver

YOUR NOTES & THOUGHTS

YOUR NOTES & THOUGHTS